LOVE, LOSS AND HIGHLAND REFLECTION

A COLLECTION OF VERSE

BY RICHARD RIDGWELL

CONTENTS

HIGHLAND INSPIRATIONS:

Elgin Cathedral..7

Sleat Old Church...8

Inverness from the Castle..10

In the Shadow of Tomnahurich...11

Craig Phadrig...12

On Loch Ness..13

Culloden Battlefield at Evening..14

Memorial Wall at Culloden Battlefield..14

A Bonnie Visitor to London, 1750..15

Churchmen of the Clearances..16

Armadale Castle..17

Badbea..17

Helmsdale..19

Glencoe in Light...20

Tavern Trail..21

A Clear Day on Meall na Teanga...22

On Stac Gorm...22

Roseisle Beach..23

NATURE:

3

The Heron………………………………..………………………………25

A Disturbance…………………………..………………………………25

The Sun's Return………………………………………………………26

Healing River……………………………………………………………27

Autumnal Respite………………………………………………………27

Late October……………………………………………………………28

POEMS OF REFLECTION:

Expectations……………………………………………………………31

Sorrow's Solace…………………………………………………………31

Cares……………………………………………………………………32

Ties that Bind……………………………………………………………33

Passing a Father Carrying His Daughter………………………………34

A Change of Plan………………………………………………………34

LOVE, HURT AND LONGING:

A Hidden Reef……………………………………………………………37

River of Desire…………………………………………………………38

Unrequited………………………………………………………………39

A Lover's Sanctuary……………………………………………………40

The Three Sisters………………………………………………………40

Love's Madness…………………………………………………………42

On Viewing Gavin Hamilton's 'Achilles Lamenting the Death of Patroclus'………43

LONELINESS:

When Lonely Wins………………………………………………………45

The Ticking Clock...45

My Shadow and I...46

Plastic Indians..48

THOUGHTS ON MORTALITY:

On a Ruined Cathedral...51

A Grave Discovery...52

Robert Fergusson's Grave...53

Robert Tannahill..54

The Necropolis, Glasgow..56

A Berwick Hanging..57

Long Enough...59

A College Death...60

ABOUT MY NIECE:

Early Reports..63

Travelling to See Her...63

A Baby's Burial...64

The Parents...64

Months Later...65

Nature's Sympathy...66

A Bad Year...67

HIGHLAND INSPIRATIONS

<u>Elgin Cathedral</u>

Stone worn resonant by the footfall of its history...

Resounding steps, resounding walls: residual olden mystery.

What was cloaked by dun-robed monks within each down-drawn hood?

What secret loves and strong desires alone they understood?

Though hallowed walls and walkways cloistered them in place,

Cassocked them till sanctified within lost halls of grace,

Mortal men they were, and just as I, not wholly good nor bad:

Some well contented in their faith; others surely driven mad.

Yet their stilled bones now cannot speak, on parchment cannot write –

Could I but feel some link with them ere joining them in night.

Their towers remain whose transience time has yet to humble:

Stepping inside I'm sure of foot; imagination stumbles –

I want to see beneath the cowl of one of hundreds gone:

That hooded host of nameless dead...I cannot picture
one.

Sleat Old Church

Hanging open and rusted, her gates beckon me,

Drawing me into the ruins curiously

(Not as they crossed her threshold, Sgitheanachs of old,

To sit there and hear their damnation unfold) –

Their pews are all gone now, a shed stands instead:

Worship's fabulous trimmings and altar have fled.

Thus by Man's hand unaided, God's work grows alone:

Should you behold the careworn walls you'd fancy that
they groan

As impressively oppressed, two tonnes of ivy billow
wide,

Though I'm little less impressed as I closer keek inside:

The landlord has an eye for comfort, the carpet's soft and
clean,

Spread across from wall to wall in myriad shades of green;

As an elaborate ceiling, in magnificent array,

An ever-changing skylight where clouds and comets play...

But soon my musing's led astray, as fluttering around,

Hop by little hop, something rustles leaf-strewn ground:

A solitary tenant inquires of his first new guest for years,

And flitting thus and bobbing, oddly helps allay old fears:

I know my fate must be to perish, and so bury me – the end;

And yet I hope, I pray to God, don't leave me with no friend:

May as restless a robin as roosts in old Sleat Church

One day find *my* resting place as comfortable a perch.

Inverness from the Castle

The cityscape's besteepled shape
Beguilingly spires the sky;
Her river shivers with delight:
Its breadth pleases my eye.
I hear the bells in joyous knells
Echo o'er the water wide –
It seems to me the city tells
The world of Highland pride.
If only the sun would always shine
On this adopted home of mine,
So just as clearly as I hear
Cathedral-pealing in my ear,
I'd see the silent distant brows
Of every hill clear sight allows,
Whose dark and hazy outlines seem
So much akin to faded dream:
To that which was but could not last –
They know the present and the past.
They saw Charles Stuart's marching men

Harry the length of their Great Glen,

But stared down, impassive, from the sky –

Had they foreseen that most would die?

Flora stands here, who shares my gaze,

Perhaps shares thoughts of yesterdays:

She does not smile, just all the while

Strains hard to see her native isle.

In the Shadow of Tomnahurich

Falling snowflakes augured a wintry day

One chill early morning, as I made my way

And was drawn to the hill that was stood on my right

In its soft halo of grey morning light...

I dreamt away from this mortal plane,

Whilst day began in muted strain –

And though no fairy folk lingered abroad

To give away their brethren's horde,

I was tempted to think of nymph and faun

Long before the auspices of dawn,

A-courting and dancing on the hill

Whose human captives must lie still:

Unable to stop, at their last porch,

Fairy kind at its nightly debauch.

My mind-conjured images grew more sinister:

Naked dryads sported on tombs of ministers,

And all the Christians who laid there for rest,

Their monuments now game for elven jest!

Although it was only my thoughts that strayed,

These images on my mind so preyed

That when I am buried, do lay me apart

From the fairy hill with the devilish heart!

Craig Phadrig

The forest abounds with all nature of sounds,

Of nestlings and wind through the trees;

As I stride up its hill

Branches buffer the chill,

Leaving a blessed breeze.

A solemn thought, how this Pictish fort

Once stood here in defiance;

As I circle its sill

All's so quiet and still,
I sorrow at its compliance.

I then sit down to rest and try my best
To shape these thoughts in words;
However, they still
Seem fashioned but ill,
Compared with the songs of the birds.

<u>On Loch Ness</u>

A funnel scythes Loch Ness in twain,
Cruising down the Highland main:
Splits shadow-darkened northern slopes
From the south's clear weather hopes.

The breakers, too,
Black left, right blue,
Seem to clarify life so clearly:
Like hope and like pain,
Dark and light will remain
Around me daily and yearly.

Culloden Battlefield at Evening

Don't the people here who walk their dogs
Think on the tragic contents of these bogs?
How many generations have to pass,
As year by year grass grows on grass,
For the silent men beneath the stones
To be dismissed as soulless bones?

Memorial Wall at Culloden Battlefield

There is not one metre's space
Upon this wall's impassive face,
With which to separate foe from foe
Where bricks of equal bareness show:
To the left, poverty-line soldiers
Fated that day to grow no older;
To the right, mixed Jacobites
Who gave their lives for Charlie's rights –
Why not compare the closest two?

It's apt they share the same stone hue:

Though representing each a man

By ideology forced to stand

Facing on Drummossie Moor

To settle cousins' royal score.

Were not both fashioned in mother's womb,

Then doomed to rot in moorland tomb?

Both hewn from the self-same stone:

From sinew and flesh, blood and bone –

Was he the one who slew the other?

Hacked life from his Earth-born brother?

Did cruel coincidence impart

A bayonet through a kinsman's heart?

It's fitting the stones, placed together, reside,

As silent memorials to leaders' pride.

A Bonnie Visitor to London, 1750

I wonder, on that London street,

How many eyes his one did meet –

That wild and yet wine-deadened eye –
Inside an eye-patched royal spy.

Could they have ever even guessed
That their gaze had come to rest
On one whose good and evil ways
Had utterly changed the nation's days?

Churchmen of the Clearances

Flocks of men for flocks of sheep:
How could they get a moment's sleep?
For even a single, conscious second?
Such 'men of God' were never beckoned
To a Lord above who omnipotent sees
'Cross burns and mountains, through the trees,
Man's inhumanity to his brother –
Our mortal lives beget no other;
So why then, if you had the chance,
Sell your soul for just a manse?

Armadale Castle

Sad Gothic pile,
Where now the smile
You wielded in your youth?
Grim-faced facade of empty looks,
You mirror now those favoured books
Of romance over truth
That your Lord loved above his clan –
Above his debtor's pride –
The Debtors' Prison lost a man
When, cloaked in chieftain's hide,
The borrower stole from kith and kin
Across th' Atlantic foam;
No begging was too low for him
To build his shame-gilt home.

Badbea*

Softly quiet laps the sea,
Quiet's all there seems to be;
Quiet-haunted is the day:
It is in all that I survey.

Quiet waltzes willing grasses
Giddily like maiden lasses
In its breezy cèilidh dance:
Silence holds them all entranced.

Quiet rides on winds that bear
Silent seabirds through the air:
Unnaturally it rules the ground
On which we sit and all around.

Quiet our tones in conversation
As we respond to this our station,
Which once knew such different noises:
Running feet and children's voices;
Hens that clucked and goats that bleated;
Here people were in Gaelic greeted.

Now there's so little left to say:
Only quiet did not leave Badbea.

"bat-bay"

Helmsdale

The grey-sky mantle suits her well,
Given the tale she has to tell.

A clock, which marks the quarter-hours
From its gloomy granite tower
Could not stand in solid grey
Had she known far better days.
How apt time's passing echoes loud,
Reminding all the mortal crowd
Of quarter-hours her soldiers lost
In Death's great harvests: human cost.

Other still figures, too in grey,
Stand aloft her barren bay,
Whose bleak unfeeling iron eyes
Seem to scan the steely skies
To far across the glass-grey sea
Where Scotia's children came to be –
Or facing backwards to the known,

See banishment from Highland home...

How odd this sombre little place
Yet leaves upon my heart a trace,
So I'd rejoice to be once more
Here when sun lies at her door.

Glencoe in Light

The Pap gleams and shimmers in unbidden light –
Leven ripples shine, now free of day's night,
Tombs sprout sharp shadows on Eilean Munde*...
Until once more the idyll sinks under
A grey-soaked dullard Highland haze
That I accept of summer days.
But as I've grown to realise
By the witness of my eyes,
We living get glimpses, but fleeting, impermanent –
It's the saintly who linger in heavenly firmament:
The light merely echoed the ethereal plain
Where those we have loved will live again.

*"ellen munder"

20

Tavern Trail

Shadow walk,
Shimmering path,
Moonlight streams
Down quiet strath…
Finger-shadowed
Cross-stitch trail
Leads me to
A pint of ale.
Sentinel peaks
Aloft surround;
No one speaks
To spoil sounds
Of trickling streams,
As Glencoe seems
Pure black-and-white:
A sacred night.
But a Clachaig glow,
Both warm and low,
Shows three friends
Their journey ends.

A Clear Day on Meall na Teanga*

God defies me with Creation
As cloud-humbled I stand
On perhaps the finest station
A view of Scotland to command:
Here atop Meall na Teanga,
Impudent tongue of the land,
He raises me up, a sinful beggar,
To be closer to His hand.

* *"mee-owl nuh chegguh"*

On Stac Gorm

My tight-locked eyes shut out the breeze,
Contented to lose all place:
High over the fields with toy-town trees
I lose the human race.

Oh let me be a wind-whipped branch,

Leaf-ravaged in a storm:

Rooted in defiant stance,

Awaiting peace and dawn.

Roseisle Beach

A Norfolk childhood's nose and ears

Billow inside 'gainst tight-shut eyes,

Bridging the wilderness of years

With sounds and smells the beach supplies

That take him back to little feet

And smaller hands sifting sand:

The adult wishes he could retreat

Into the memory that leaves him unmanned.

<u>NATURE</u>

The Heron

By his island, safely moated,
Stands the Heron, patience-coated;
Across the water Man hurries by,
But cannot disturb his fish-trained eye –
Yet one Adam's son, as he vainly scribbles,
Alerts the watcher of river's ripples:
One misplaced foot, one brittle stick,
Familiar sounds so carelessly pricked –
Then a water-steeped hop from spindled limbs
Sees the Lord of the Isle take to his wings...
Leaving the poet to think once again
On the gulf between creatures and ignorant men.

A Disturbance

To my left and to my right
The hedge reverberates with fright:
The placid scene that late was found
Disturbed by boots on heavy ground.

Winged inhabitants, more than few,
Embursting outwards, meet our view –
A minute passes; then again
The birds retake their peaceful den.

The Sun's Return

Ficklest mistress of the sky,
I can't despise you, though I try
To reprimand your absence daily,
You return so bright and gaily:
Airily you excuse yourself –
You flitsome, flightsome, maddening elf!
Love so inconstant never took
Quite so unashamed a look
As when your marble shines aloft –
My world was hard; it now is soft
With greenery of every shade
As leaves reflect what God has made.
The clouds you dallied with have flown,
And once again you're mine alone.

Healing River

The river's revels

So bedevil

The agony inside,

They bursts the banks

As I with thanks

Cast anguish far and wide.

Each care is but a ripple

That I mark with my eye,

Until all cares are crippled

And harmlessly float by.

Autumnal Respite

Light transparent through the leaves,

Lightly twitched by barely breeze,

Casts a lightsome shadow down:

Autumn cheers the matted ground.

Even the browns so summer red
That I forget the matter's dead,
Long fallen from the barely trees:
I fain would have more days like these.

Late October

Petulant Autumn's restless refrain
Wreaks vengeance on my view again:
The very green's robbed from the leaves
As, discontented, on she thieves:
Withering all the sweetest flowers,
Inflicting her tithe on daybright hours;
For compensation paints muted hues,
Premeditating Winter's blues –
Of a sudden Springtime radiates by,
For a fresh-faced maiden meets my eye,
And though Autumn, jealous, vents her spleen,
Her gusts faze not this May-time queen;
Yet she too will see her seasons changed,

Her youthful beauty disarranged...
Such sobering thoughts afflict my day:
Are we just here to grow, decay?
But such October ruminations
Stifle Man's best machinations,
And I know for sure our mortal scope
Offers much to give those aging hope:
A beautiful woman's still one to prize,
As I shall ever while I've eyes;
Children at disport unawares
How they alleviate my cares;
The satisfaction of work well done:
These things are found beneath the sun.
The future may be dark, but only Heaven knows
Where Man's soul, like his Summertime, goes.

POEMS OF REFLECTION

Expectations

Can a soul be pressed by pen onto a naked page?

Can everything we think ourselves be laid out stage by
stage?

Poets Tennyson and Burns, in stanzas soft but clear,

Told once-empty manuscripts their every hope and fear.

Should I be cowed by genius, doubt-laden hold my
tongue?

Men like these created work: where does this fool's
belong?

Yet like a Bible-studied child who has been shown the
way,

I will ensure my faltering steps shall see the light of day.

Sorrow's Solace

When sorrow savages with rabid teeth
I press a pen into my hand;
As the poison seeps its way beneath
I'll need my firebrand.

To cauterise the heinous wounds, I write into the raw –

Take a deep look down inside myself, then open up
some more:

The more I expose to the light,

The more I must despair;

Yet as the paper hears my plight,

Life's easier to bear.

Cares

Our greatest worries, sight unseen,

We keep in heart and mind;

We show them not, the outer screen,

The visage we all feel behind,

Helps obscure the hurt and weight

That we so tire of bearing;

Yet though we often think we hate

The burdening of our lives,

It's in the weight of love and caring

Man's humanity thrives;

For if our families were not there –

And no friends we had to cry for –

What left in life but emptiness,

Ourselves and nothing more?

Ties that Bind

Some ties that bind you cannot find
By nearness on the tree:
Closest descent I'll not consent
Must mean much more to me,
For love is found in fellowship true
Across the human race;
Though unrelated I to you,
I need not keep your place
Far apart from a family chart
That threatens to dictate,
In my life the players' parts,
And not the hand of Fate.
For you, friend, are as close to me
As flesh and blood my own:
We are two ones in sympathy,
Need never feel alone.

Passing a Father Carrying His Daughter

His world upon his shoulders,
The father stoops to give
His world a better view of
The world in which they live;
And his little daughter's little hands –
Her little eyes and feet –
Give his world dimensions
In edges soft and sweet.

A Change of Plan

Recoiling from the precipice
That overhung the dark abyss,
I staggered, fell, in such a way –
When I came to, it was bright day.

Then Sense returned, and little Hope:
The almost-orphans I betrayed,
Who dragged me some way up the slope –
And from the final plans I'd made.

Their worthless father they forgave,

Though he was not deserving –

They kept him from the darkened grave,

Thought life was worth preserving.

LOVE, HURT AND LONGING

A Hidden Reef

Her soft corroding tears seep under

As without reprieve he's torn asunder;

Were there no others she could have met

Whilst her lovely eyes were brimming wet?

But she happened on him, a hapless friend,

Who couldn't know how his heart she would rend.

So it was his lot to be lost and then grounded,

Before "Hard to port!" could ever be sounded;

Yet holding her, her slender frame,

He lost all meaning, even shame:

Nothing mattered as weeping she pressed

Him against her dearest breast.

How close he came to telling all –

To setting out his squalid stall –

To telling one so in love with another:

He thought her sister, but was no brother –

Had only believed that at the start,
Before he knew his traitorous heart.

So though single, though he was free,
Could roam wherever he wanted to be,
When anchored fast at night, a-bed,
Thoughts of her still breached his head.

Haunted, he missed nocturnal noise,
For there was nought to mute her voice
As it lulled and cajoled, wouldn't be quieted
Till bitter but sweetly he'd fall benighted.

Thrice-innocent siren, she must never know
How he longs again to hold her so.

River of Desire

I drape her happy by a river,
Pour sunshine on her head;
And so from pain I'm thus delivered,
Though feverously lovesick in bed.

How clear her image: maiden fair,

With unashamed smile like day;

I bless her softly dangling hair

As currents hold it in sway...

Jealous am I of that lucky water,

Though grasping its riches so lightly –

If it were I instead who had caught her,

I'd cherish her so much more tightly.

Unrequited

Actions like Judas betray me,

Though I mustn't admit my shame;

Yet even voice betrays me,

Every mention of her name.

Why did I have to meet her then, when her heart was
close to breaking?

Why couldn't I have met her when her heart was free for
taking?

I long to hold her in my arms, and pledge a lover's
plight,

But try stopping desire with moral qualms:

It's as simple as stopping the night.

A Lover's Sanctuary

After parting let me reside
Where I may nurse my love-worn hide:
In some sea-cave oceans batter –
I alone, my heart in tatters.
I'd spread its shreds upon the floor,
Rest on them, some warmth to draw,
But little comfort would be found
There on my unhallowed ground.
At least, though, lost there to the world,
Safe-harboured from a once-loved girl.

The Three Sisters

Love, close sister of Loss and Pain,
Is daring me to care again;
Yet there is nothing I want more
Than to chain the casket, lock the door,
Hurl all feeling in the sea,
So long as love can't darken me.

What utter bliss to be thus free,
Without feelings left inside of me,
As lost amongst incurious fish,
Safely sunk in dark abyss,
I'd leave them on that ocean floor,
So long as I should love no more.

But Love stuck to her deadly art:
Taunted, twitched, a rotting heart –
Then thrust her hand into its core,
Scarring it putrid, bloodied, raw:
The physical pain I could easily bear,
So long as love remained not there.

Then Loss and Pain in triumph appeared –
How they pranced, and danced, and jeered!
Each grasped my heart's bared visceral strands,
Tearing them out me with merciless hands:
Yet I fretted not for damage done,
So long as love could ne'er return.

But then fresh cruelty, unabated,
Saw flesh and blood regenerated,
Till dying whilst living I broke on the floor,
Screaming and begging to feel no more;

Then my heart longed for but a knife,
So long as love would leave with life.

Love's Madness

To hell with love and all its madness,
I'm through with love, twice sick of sadness
That time and again leaves me distressed,
Deprived of sense I once possessed.

Could I but learn to cool these veins
To ebb and flow in calmer strains,
Then never again should I be shamed
By a head and heart at once inflamed
With this unquenchable boyish desire
To bathe you in their white-hot fire.

If it weren't heart but head that ruled,
Heart could be learnéd, better schooled:
Could read all the signs, and work out that you
Must be avoided, lest he be cloven anew.

On Viewing Gavin Hamilton's 'Achilles Lamenting the Death of Patroclus'

Ready deified, the alabaster dead

Finds homage from the multitude

That crowds his bleachéd statue head,

Reclined in languished attitude

Upon love's lap, greyed tresses lying

Lightly on Achilles' strength;

It is a friend and lover's dying

Will see the latter, too, at length,

Fallen on Homeric pages,

For no mortal conquers all:

A sad example for the ages

How true love leads to man's fall.

<u>LONELINESS</u>

When Lonely Wins

When loneliness assails your days,
Don't hide beneath your casement:
Allow its euthanasiac ways
Inside from crown to basement;
Only when it's scooped you out,
And left your insides bare –
When zombie-like you drift about,
With no feelings left to care –
Then neither winter's bitter darts,
Nor summer's mocking gladness,
Can ever harm your stony heart,
Safe petrified by sadness.

The Ticking Clock

Tick little clock, tick out the hours,
Second upon second –

A little task and yet your powers

Are more than I had reckoned.

A sad succession of answer tones

Has burrowed deep into my bones;

Days and weeks, and months and years,

Are answering all my deepest fears:

That I must live through life alone –

Aging by a silent phone.

My Shadow and I

I took my shadow for a walk,

So I'd not be alone;

And we engaged in idle talk

Ere heading back for home.

Though on the way we lingered while

We took a little drink –

And, oh! How he could make me smile

At what he'd say and think;

Yet most unusually, that day

A woman talked to me:

Shadow kindly faded grey,
So none but her I'd see.

I paid her many compliments,
Paid for her drinks and more,
And in happy consequence
I spun her round the floor;
I danced the best dance that I can,
There where the music blared:
But when she saw a better man
How sorry I was I cared.

Yet shadow saw, came back again,
As discreetly as he left,
So as she flirted with those men
I wouldn't feel bereft
Of kindness, friendship, company:
I had no need to grieve;
Though when they turned to stare at me
I knew we two must leave.

But why these tears in my eyes?
What their mocking looks to me?
Yet then outside, in night's disguise,

Shadow too took leave of me.

Plastic Indians

Mere boy he was, but how he played –
Like the Indians' fortress he dismayed;
And oh, what fun! To think of how
The sand must clog up every mouth,
Stopping each and every breath:
Causing them an awful death.
Boy revelled in his barbarous act;
He knew full well, a certain fact:
A god was he, could imagine again
Life back into murdered men;
But boy, ever careless, never spied
The insidious seeping of the tide...
With horror, seeing his grave mistake,
The Indians' grave began to rake –
But though he fain would stop to linger,
Boy-buried Indians slipped his fingers.
Mother dragged him, crying, home to tea...
All of his Indians washed out by the sea.

Boy grew up, grew smarter, thought he;

But, in truth, no wiser to be.

His Indians forgotten, he now played games

With toys of very different names:

Jessica, Laura, Jane and more

Filled his heart's revolving door...

Should he lose one, another he'd get,

With barely, if even, an hour of regret.

But the tide still came on, and sandbanks it brought –

Though the boy, now a man, gave time's passage no
thought –

Until surrounded and stranded, single was he...

With all of his Indians washed out by the sea.

THOUGHTS ON MORTALITY

On a Ruined Cathedral

Weathered faces, emptied spaces,
Time missed nothing here –
No sacred nook could safely brook
The worsening of years:
No stained glass pane, no altar,
No finely carved ramparts;
Time's cruelty never faltered,
Broke a hundred bishops' hearts.

Weathered faces, empty spaces,
Agéd stone a knight encases:
Where now all his knightly graces?
No features he now bears:
No furrow on his manly brow
Survives until our Godless now,
No mark of grief or care.
He served his king, his God above,
Where now his stone-carved parts?

Where the man whose courtly love
Broke a hundred maidens' hearts?

A Grave Discovery

I never saw a grave in chains,
Not till that wintry season
I happed on rusted iron remains,
Without apparent reason
Strangling the very stone
Deep-etched with family names;
And as I stood there all alone,
I thought it cruellest shame.
Such uncommon sight all made,
Snow billowing around:
Encircling that aged grave
On consecrated ground.
How my thoughts, they eddied too,
For some natural solution;
Yet all seemed eerie, quite untrue:
Sacrilegious the pollution.
No pessimism haunted graves
Within its close vicinity –
They believed in He who saves:

In Godhead and Divinity.

Perhaps some kin, whilst sore effaced

By some imagined slight,

Around the tomb such barrier placed

To keep them from the Light?

What fleeting things those metal rings,

To ward off the immortal –

They waste like us, decay like us,

They cannot close the portal!

Robert Fergusson's Grave

How long it's been, two hundred years,

Since genius wet with earnest tears

A simple patch of unmarked earth,

And swore to show the poet's worth.

Edina's sons should recognise

One of theirs in Canongate lies,

Who inspired Burns in Scots to write –

To them bequeathing each Burns Night –

And should they want their city's history,

Its lives and loves are little mystery:
Their boy poet captured, from the street,
The common sights that he would meet:
From 'The King's Birth-Day' to the 'Tron-Kirk Bell',
As he rhymed and satirised equally well.

I try to linger as torrents abound,
Mingling with his sodden ground,
But earthly troubles fog my brain:
I have to catch the northbound train.
Hurriedly reading out his lines,
Emitting only wind-drowned whines,
I have no time for weeping,
So leave the poor boy sleeping;
His 'Daft Days' may have long since passed,
But I heartily wish his legacy would last.

Robert Tannahill

Gloom-threaded loom the poet plied,

With song he interlaced
To counter all the pain inside,
The drudgery he faced.
The many threads of sorrow's woes
Entwined about his stricken being:
Inflicted such depressive throes
From which there was no fleeing.

Tannahill, you pitiable soul!
How you suffered I comprehend:
I too have felt devoured whole,
Tormented without end.

The merciful Maxwelton Burn
Absolved you of your pain:
But that meant you could not return,
Your loom not sing again.

Black Peter fished the sodden leaf,
Hard-fallen from the branch of life;
The act had granted you release,
And cost a good friend's strife.

Although I shall not gain your fame,

I hope much older to survive:

Suffering melancholic pain

That I interweave with life.

The Necropolis, Glasgow

All who lie here once were loved,

And sombre monuments built above

Seem to petition to God from Earth

In enormity, their incumbents' worth;

But carved angels rotting round the frames

Speak silent stone of mortal fames,

Here where no one bows their head,

And statues mourn the myriad dead –

Where only a handful of tourists pry

Ornate devotions to the sky.

Long-lost mourners now make home

Beneath the soft and mossy loam

Of other Glasgow graveyard sites,
To deprive this place its graveside rites:
No fresh flowers' irreligious colour
Can interrupt the dull and duller
On this mournful Glasgow hill
Knox towers proud to preach o'er still.

A Berwick Hanging

One July day they hanged Grace Griffin
On a scaffold of indifferent trees
That stood there till her limbs had stiffened –
Till nothing stirred her save the breeze;
But the gallows had no knowledge of
The man who beat her to her knees.

Two weeks one time he'd laid her down
A full fortnight in bed,
She couldn't limp up to the town,
Could barely lift her head;
For her sake and her children's
She had left the drunkard dead.

No judge could sway the vengeful jury,
Cries for clemency went unheeded,
For self-righteous mobs' unthinking fury
Is ever deaf to what is pleaded;
Alone and afraid, a poor woman
Saw so clearly her hopes were defeated.

Yet as she faced her baying crowd,
Though timid, she held her head high:
Not by them would Grace Griffin be cowed,
Not though she walked out to die –
She looked beyond the angry mob
To see the bright blue of the sky.

Her eyes took in the twinkling Tweed,
Its glittering sweep round the hill,
Whose majesty answered her direst need:
To give her some warmth from the chill,
So cold were the looks of the people
Who gathered below for the kill.

Some who were there could understand
The plight of her they came to see:
They knew of drunken husbands' hands,

Of misery and poverty;
But still they came to gawk at
Grace dance on the gallows tree.

Long Enough

Long enough to envy youth,
To hide away from mortal truths:
Just long enough to realise
You've been the butt of self-told lies.

Long enough to see the end –
To die yourself or lose old friends –
Just long enough to take your time,
Then bitterly repent the crime.

Long enough to veer between
Popularity and low esteem:
Just long enough to watch decay
And dream too much of yesterday.

Long enough to feel you're wise

And then regret the rash surmise;

Just long enough to see it plain:

You were the cause of others' pain.

Long enough to live and breathe

Until in death you find reprieve;

Just long enough for years of strife:

Just long enough, an adult life.

A College Death

Three bookmarked books upon the floor, which no more
would be read;

An empty glass beside the door, last placed there by the
dead:

It had played its humane part, delivered him from
himself,

And yet looked no more guilty than those stood upon the
shelf.

The mortuary, still so new, showed signs of recent life –

See the crumbs upon the plate, see the unwashed knife;

See mother's picture on the wall, smiling unaware

That the son she beams upon is now no longer there.

As a life is stripped from walls and draws, a cleaner
heaves a sigh:
She only knew the what of it, she didn't know the why.
A dead man's loves and nameless fears he takes into his
grave,
And of all his earthbound schemes leaves nothing left to
save.

The room itself, in blameless white, gets mothballed for
its crime,
Then for one semester it in silence bides its time...
For several more that numbered door is kept from being
lonely:
Reserved in exclusivity for stays of short-term only.

Yet when all had left the hall who knew of its sad
history,
It opened up to others who were ignorant of its mystery,
But the legend lingered as legends do, without
understanding –
Was it 203 or 202? Didn't they find him on the landing?

The real truth was so banal, the way they'd found him
lying,

Though it galled them even more to see the way that
he'd been crying

Tears onto a pillow, into which no more would seep –

But with eyes wide open, he'd at last found peace in
sleep.

ABOUT MY NIECE

Early Reports

Fate says she'll not see two winters;
Look at my heart, then count its splinters.

My brother's love has been chastised:
Take from him his first-born, prized
Above all else, even life,
Take her from him and his wife.

Were they too faithful or too pure,
He too loyal, she demure?
What excuse could ever be made
To a family love by life betrayed?

Don't ever tell me it's 'God's Will'
When a blameless baby is cold and still.

Travelling to See Her

Rain is coming, over my train then across the land;
Pain is coming, the baby's death so close at hand:
That cloud-black ceiling choking the sky

Mirrors my feelings; I try not to cry.

Soon water appears that eases the skies,
As tears must dry out weeping eyes;
It clears: God kept his olden promise,
So sun reveals His shred of solace.

Dark though the clouds were, I will live with the pain,
For life, like the land, is sometimes needful of rain.

A Baby's Burial

The little root lies in the ground, but it never flowers;
Though growing such a little time, we'll not forget she's
ours.

The Parents

Guiltless babe, what died with thee?
A little of their every days.
Although on land they wander free,
Their actions seem suited to plays:

Enter right, a mourner wearied,
Through his office motions goes –
Enter left, a mother blearied
From sleepless nights, half-comatose.
They smile on cue, when needed they nod,
As social customs ask,
But sore entombed within the sod
Their hearts lie in that cask.
The whys, the whys, those stubborn cries
Of an ordered world they knew...
All are lost when a baby dies
And takes a part of you.
Then there aren't answers to impart,
Death's verdict has been given;
Nothing to salve their love-raw hearts
When from her they've been riven.

Months Later

Green leaves are crying in the garden rain –
I cannot tell whether for joy or for sorrow –
Teardrops are sticking to the window-pane...
Resting my head, I count empty tomorrows.

The rain falls on a tiny grave, many miles away,

And grass weeps in sympathy with fresh-fallen dew:

The little grass-blades have the decency to pray,

As the tears of the sky bend them closer to you.

Nature's Sympathy

From grey of May to gloom in June,

July dismay and August ruined:

It's been so dull since your death, little one –

I wonder, is it that which has clouded the sun?

Colour-drained and sepia-toned,

Summer here has been postponed,

And seems to reflect in sober awning

That nature too is quietly mourning

The loss of the best who was never to roam

So much as the nursery floor:

May light illume her ethereal home

So one day I can find its door.

A Bad Year

I still remember last September
Another wore this name;
Strange but true how that other, too,
Bore exactly identical frame.
But the bounce in step and ready grin –
It was not me, that other him –
The sunny shadow of my skin.
For a heart twice broken
Thrice slowly must heal,
And love once it's spoken
Cannot be repealed;
Had I not seen one loved girl dying,
Would it have easier been?
Had I not seen one loved girl crying,
Would my heart have been safe-screened?
All I know is something was lost,
And now I twice must count the cost.
How I long to revisit that former man...
He lived life better than I can.